SUPER
SIMPLE
ORIGAMI

ORIGAMI
FARM ANIMALS

Easy & Fun Paper-Folding Projects

Anna George

Consulting Editor, Diane Craig, M.A./Reading Specialist

Super Sandcastle

An Imprint of Abdo Publishing
abdopublishing.com

abdopublishing.com

Published by Abdo Publishing, a division of ABDO, PO Box 398166, Minneapolis, Minnesota 55439.
Copyright © 2017 by Abdo Consulting Group, Inc. International copyrights reserved in all countries.
No part of this book may be reproduced in any form without written permission from the publisher.
Super SandCastle™ is a trademark and logo of Abdo Publishing.

Printed in the United States of America, North Mankato, Minnesota
102016
012017

THIS BOOK CONTAINS
RECYCLED MATERIALS

Editor: Liz Salzmann
Content Developer: Nancy Tuminelly
Cover and Interior Design and Production: Mighty Media, Inc.
Photo Credits: iStockphoto; Mighty Media, Inc.; Shutterstock
Special Thanks to Kazuko Collins

The following manufacturers/names appearing in this book are trademarks: Elmer's® Glue-All®

Publisher's Cataloging-in-Publication Data
Names: George, Anna, author.
Title: Origami farm animals: easy & fun paper-folding projects / by Anna George.
Other titles: Easy & fun paper-folding projects | Easy and fun paper-folding projects
Description: Minneapolis, MN : Abdo Publishing, 2017. | Series: Super simple origami
Identifiers: LCCN 2016944710 | ISBN 9781680784480 (lib. bdg.) |
    ISBN 9781680798012 (ebook)
Subjects: LCSH: Domestic animals in art--Juvenile literature. | Origami--Juvenile
    literature.| Paper work--Juvenile literature. | Handicraft--Juvenile literature.
Classification: DDC 736/.982--dc23
LC record available at http://lccn.loc.gov/2016944710

Super SandCastle™ books are created by a team of professional educators, reading specialists, and
content developers around five essential components—phonemic awareness, phonics, vocabulary, text
comprehension, and fluency—to assist young readers as they develop reading skills and strategies and
increase their general knowledge. All books are written, reviewed, and leveled for guided reading and
early reading intervention programs for use in shared, guided, and independent reading and writing
activities to support a balanced approach to literacy instruction.

CONTENTS

AMAZING ORIGAMI FARM ANIMALS

Origami is the art of folding paper. In Japanese, the word *ori* means "to fold" and *gami* means "paper." People in Japan and all around the world enjoy origami.

Do you have a favorite farm animal? Is it a cow? Or maybe a pig? This book will show you how to make those animals and more! These super simple origami projects are great for beginners. You will learn about:

> ▶ different types of paper folds
>
> ▶ **symbols** used in origami **diagrams**
>
> ▶ types of paper that will work for origami

You'll be **amazed** at what you can make with just one sheet of paper!

BASIC FOLDS

MOUNTAIN FOLD
Fold behind to create a mountain.

VALLEY FOLD
Fold in front to create a valley.

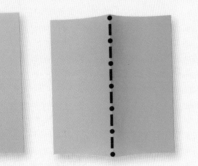

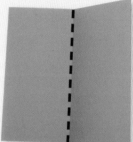

CREASE
Fold and unfold to make a **crease**.

ORIGAMI SYMBOLS

The **symbols** below show the most common actions used in origami.

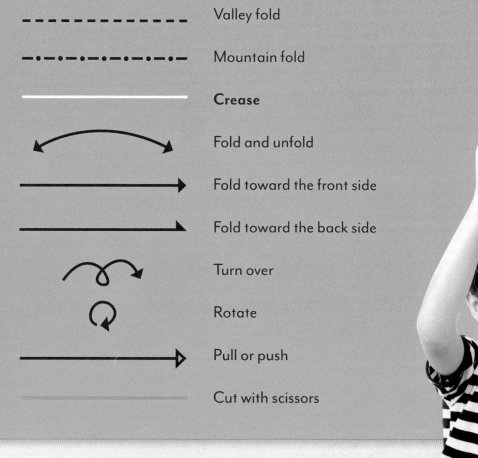

- - - - - - - - - - - -	Valley fold
-·-·-·-·-·-·-·-	Mountain fold
———————	**Crease**
⌒→	Fold and unfold
——————→	Fold toward the front side
——————▷	Fold toward the back side
↷	Turn over
↻	Rotate
——————▷	Pull or push
———————	Cut with scissors

SPECIAL FOLDS

INSIDE REVERSE FOLD

This fold is often used to make the head or feet of an animal.
It may seem hard at first. After you practice it will become easier.
Here are instructions to make this fold.

1

Fold a square piece of
paper into a triangle. Valley
fold one of the points.

2

Crease it firmly.
Unfold.

3

Mountain fold the
crease. Unfold.

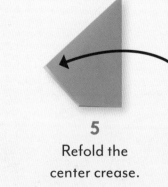

4

Unfold the paper. Place it so the
center crease is vertical. Valley
fold the bottom point.

5

Refold the
center crease.

OUTSIDE REVERSE FOLD

This fold is often used to make the head of a bird or the feet of an animal. It is just like the inside **reverse** fold except the corner is folded on the outside.

1
Fold a square piece of paper into a triangle. Valley fold one of the points.

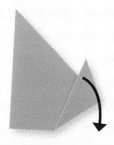

2
Crease it firmly. Unfold.

3
Mountain fold the crease. Unfold.

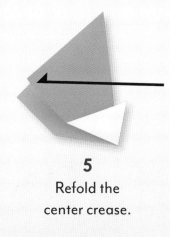

4
Unfold the paper and turn it over. Place it so the center crease is vertical. Valley fold the bottom point.

5
Refold the center crease.

BASES

These shapes are used as bases for many different origami models. Practicing these will help you improve your origami.

SQUARE BASE

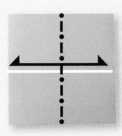 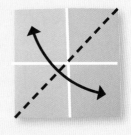 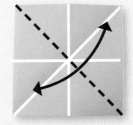

1
Place the paper on the table with a straight edge at the top. Mountain fold the top to the bottom. Unfold.

2
Mountain fold the right side to the left side. Unfold.

3
Valley fold one point to the opposite point. Unfold.

4
Valley fold the other two points together. Unfold.

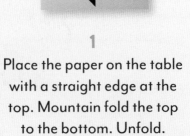  

5
Pinch and lift two opposite mountain folds.

6
Press the sides together.

7
Flatten the paper into a square.

BIRD BASE

1

Start with a square base.
Place it with the open
point at the bottom.

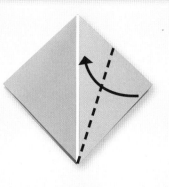

2

Valley fold the top
layer of the right point
to the center **crease**.

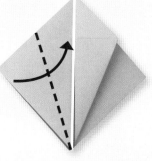

3

Valley fold the top
layer of the left point
to the center crease.

4

Valley fold the top point
down. Unfold the last
three folds you made.

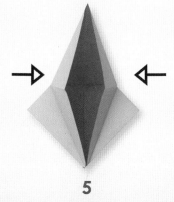

5

Lift the top layer of the
bottom point. Push the sides
together. Flatten the sides.

6

Turn the model over from
side to side. Repeat steps
2 through 5.

MATERIALS

BONE FOLDER

CRAFT STICK

PAPER

You can use almost any type of paper for origami. You can get special origami paper at craft stores or online. You can also use copy paper, magazine pages, scrapbooking paper, and even gift wrap!

CREASING TOOLS

The edge of a ruler, craft stick, or bone folder can help you make good **creases** and folds.

SCISSORS

You will need scissors if you are starting with a sheet of paper that isn't square. (See page 13.)

EXTRAS

These are **optional** supplies used in this book.

- googly eyes
- glue
- markers
- cotton ball

ELMER'S
Glue-All
Multi-Purpose

TIPS AND TRICKS

GET SQUARE

Many origami models use a square piece of paper.
It is easy to make a rectangular piece of paper square.

1 Fold one short edge so it lines up with a long edge.
Crease the fold.

2 Cut off the strip under the triangle.

3 Unfold the paper. Now you have a square!

PRACTICE MAKES PERFECT!

When folding origami models, it is important for the folds to be as **accurate** as possible. Match up the edges and corners when folding. Make firm creases. The more folds there are, the more important it is to make them exact. So get out some scrap paper and practice, practice, practice!

YELLOW CHICK

- yellow paper (square)
- googly eyes
- glue

1

Place the paper on the table with a point at the top. The side facing down should be yellow.

2

Valley fold the top point to the bottom point.

3

Valley fold each side point to the bottom point.

4

Mountain fold the left point to the right point.

5

Make an inside **reverse** fold on the top point to form the beak. (See page 8.)

6

Valley fold the top layer of the bottom point. The point should stick out above the edge.

7

Turn the model over from side to side. Repeat the valley fold on the other side.

8

Glue a googly eye to each side of the head.

SHEEP FACE

- paper (square)
- googly eyes
- glue
- cotton balls
- scissors
- marker

1

Place the paper on the table with a point at the top. Your sheep will be the color of the facedown side.

2

Valley fold the top point to the bottom point.

3

Valley fold the right point to the left point.

4

Valley fold the top layer of the left point. The point should stick out beyond the long side.

5

Turn the model over from side to side. Repeat the valley fold on the other layer of the point.

6

Unfold the center **crease**.
The side points are the
sheep's ears.

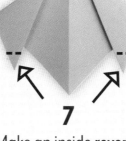

7

Make an inside **reverse**
fold on the tip of each ear.
(See page 8.)

8

Mountain fold the
bottom point.

9

Glue on the
googly eyes.

10

Cut a piece off a cotton
ball. Glue it to the head
between the ears.

11

Use the marker
to draw a nose.

17

BROWN COW

- brown paper (square)
- googly eyes
- glue
- marker

1

Place the paper on the table with a point at the top. The side facing down should be brown.

2

Valley fold the top point to the bottom point.

3

Valley fold the right and left points. The points should overlap.

4

Valley fold the left point back.

5

Valley fold the right point back.

6

Valley fold the left point up.

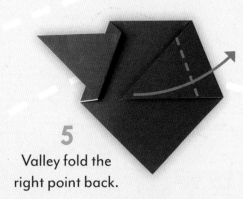

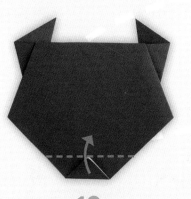

7

Valley fold the right point up. These points are the horns.

8

Turn the model over from side to side. Mountain fold the top.

9

Valley fold the bottom point.

10

Valley fold the bottom point again.

11

Unfold the two **previous** folds. Fold the bottom layer under the top layer on the second fold. Refold both folds on the top layer.

12

Glue on the googly eyes. Use the marker to draw **nostrils**.

FLOATING DUCK

- paper (square)
- googly eyes
- glue

1

Place the paper on the table with a straight edge at the top. Your duck will be the color of the facedown side.

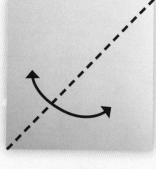

2

Valley fold the bottom right point to the top left point. Unfold.

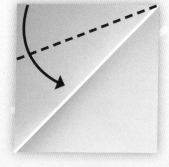

3

Valley fold the top left point to the center **crease**.

4

Valley fold the bottom right point to the center **crease**.

5

Rotate so the narrow point is at the top.

6

Valley fold the side points up to the center crease.

Continued on the next page.

7

Turn the model over from side to side. Valley fold the left point to the right point.

8

Rotate so the wide point is at the top. Make an outside **reverse** fold on the left point. (See page 9.)

9

Make a small outside reverse fold on the end of the left point. This will be the head.

11

Glue a googly
eye to each side
of the head.

10

Make a shorter
outside **reverse** fold
on the right point.

12

Open up the
bottom a bit so the
duck can stand.

PINK
PIG

- pink paper (square)
- googly eyes
- glue

1
Place the paper
on the table with
straight edge at the
top. The side facing
down should be pink.

2
Valley fold the bottom
edge to the top edge.
Unfold.

3
Valley fold the
bottom edge
to the center
crease.

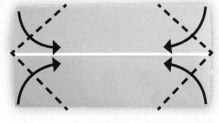

5

Valley fold each
corner point to the
center crease.

4

Valley fold
the top edge
to the center
crease.

6

Valley fold the
side points in.
Unfold.

Continued
on the
next page.

7

Mountain fold the bottom
edge to the top edge.

8

Pull the corners on the top layer
open and flatten them into
triangles. Turn the model over
from side to side. Repeat with
the corners on the other side.

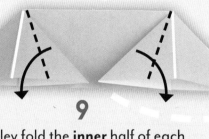

9

Valley fold the **inner** half of each
flattened triangle to the center lines.
Turn the model over from side to
side. Repeat with the triangles on the
other side. This forms the legs.

10

Make an inside **reverse** fold on one end to form the tail. (See page 8.)

11

Make a small inside reverse fold on the other end to form the **snout**.

12

Glue a googly eye to each side of the head.

HANDSOME HORSE

- paper (square)
- scissors
- googly eyes
- glue

1

Start with a square base.
(See page 10.) Set the
base on the table with the
open point at the bottom.

2

Valley fold the top
layer of the right
point up to the
center **crease**.

3

Valley fold the top layer
of the left point up to
the center crease.

4

Valley fold the top point down. Unfold the last three folds.

5

Make a cut in the top layer only along the center **crease** up to the top crease.

6

Valley fold the top layer of both sides of the point up.

Continued on the next page.

7

Valley fold the top layer of the right point to the center.

8

Valley fold the top layer of the left point to the center.

9

Turn the model over from side to side. Repeat steps 2 through 8 on the other side.

10

Rotate the model so the large point is facing up. Valley fold the upper right point at the same angle as the lower part of the left point. Unfold.

11

Make an outside **reverse** fold on the **crease**. (See page 9.) This is the tail.

12

Mountain fold the upper left point. Unfold.

13

Make an inside reverse fold on the crease. (See page 8.) This is the head.

14

Make a tiny inside reverse fold on each leg to help the horse stand.

15

Glue a googly eye to each side of the head.

GLOSSARY

accurate — exact or correct.

amaze — to surprise or fill with wonder.

crease — 1. a line made by folding something.
2. to make a sharp line in something by folding it.

diagram — a drawing that shows how something works or how parts go together.

inner — on the inside.

nostril — an opening in the nose.

optional — something you can choose, but is not required.

previous — the one or ones before.

reverse — backwards, in the opposite direction.

snout — the jaws and nose of an animal.

symbol — an object or picture that stands for or represents something.